Mel Bay's
Classical Repertoire for
VIOLIN

Volume One

By Costel Puscoiu

1 2 3 4 5 6 7 8 9 0

Visit us on the Web at http://www.melbay.com — E-mail us at email@melbay.com

CONTENTS

		Violin	Piano
Foreword		4	5
About the Author		5	7
Children's Song	W. A. Mozart	6	8
To Joy (from Symphony no. 9)	L. van Beethoven	6	8
Saint Anthony Chorale	J. Haydn	6	9
Gavotte	M. Praetorius	7	10
Fanfare	M. Corrette	7	11
Air	W. A. Mozart	7	12
Minuet	Anonymous	8	13
Gavotte	G. Fr. Händel	8	14
Oh, Tiny Child	J. S. Bach	8	15
Minuet	J. Hook	9	16
Andantino	J. B. Lully	9	17
Brunette	J. B. de Boismortier	9	17
March (from "The Peasants' Cantata)	J. S. Bach	10	18
Minuet (from "Fireworks Music")	G. Fr. Händel	10	19
Minuet (from "Fireworks Music")	G. Fr. Händel	11	20
Brandle	J. B. de Boismortier	11	21
Melody (from "Album for the Youth")	R. Schumann	11	22
Rondino	J. Ph. Rameau	12	24
Burlesque (from "Music book for Wolfgang")	L. Mozart	12	26
Scarborough Fair	Traditional	13	27
The Royal March of the Lion (from "Le carnaval des animaux")	C. Saint-Saëns	13	28
Andante	J. Haydn	13	29
Michael's Song	C. Puscoiu	14	30
English Dance	H. Purcell	14	31
Gavotte	G. Fr. Händel	15	32
Impertinence	G. Fr. Händel	15	33
Trumpet Air (from "The Indian Queen")	D. Purcell	16	34
Greensleeves	Old English song	16	34
Plaisir d'Amour	J. P. Martini	17	36
Chorale (from "Music book for Anna Magdelena Bach")	J. S. Bach	17	37
Minuet	Joh. Krieger	18	38

		Violin	Piano
Because We Are Cheerful	V. Rathgeber	18	39
Arietta	J. Haydn	19	40
Bourrée	Joh. Krieger	19	41
Minuet	G. Ph. Telemann	20	42
Andante (from Brandenburg Concerto no. 4)	J. S. Bach	20	43
Rondeau	J. B. de Boismortier	21	44
Tambourin	J. Ph. Rameau	22	46
March (from "Judas Maccabaeus")	G. Fr. Händel	22	47
Gavotte	E. Ph. Chedeville	23	48
Lullaby	Joh. Brahms	23	49
Gavotte	G. Fr. Händel	24	50
Theme from "Swan Lake"	P. I. Tchaikovsky	24	51
Lullaby	W. A. Mozart	25	52
Gavotte	A. Corelli	25	53
Waltz	Joh. Brahms	26	54
Martial Air	H. Purcell	26	56
Minuet (from "Music book for Anna Magdelena Bach")	J. S. Bach	27	58
Sarabande	A. Corelli	27	59
March (from the "Occasional Oratorio")	G. Fr. Händel	28	60
Panis Angelicus	C. Franck	29	62
Largo (from opera "Xerxes")	G. Fr. Händel	30	65
Bourrée (from Sonata no. 2 in G major)	G. Fr. Händel	30	68
Minuet (from "Music book for Anna Magdelena Bach")	J. S. Bach	31	70
Musette 1 and 2 (from Sonata "La Persane")	Ph. de Lavigne	32	72
Ave Verum	W. A. Mozart	33	74
Preludio (from Sonata in A minor)	A. Corelli	34	76
Minuet	G. Ph. Telemann	34	78
Berceuse	G. Fauré	35	80
Allegro (from Brandenburg Concerto no. 5)	J. S. Bach	36	82
Vivace (from Sonata in D major)	J. B. Loeillet de Gant	36	83
The Peace (from "Fireworks Music")	G. Fr. Händel	38	86
Allegro (from Brandenburg Concerto no. 1)	J. S. Bach	38	88
Träumerei (from "Chindren's scenes")	R. Schumann	39	90
Polovetsian Dance (from opera "Tsar Igor")	A. Borodin	40	92

FOREWORD

In 1991 I brought out the first edition of my "CLASSICAL REPERTOIRE FOR PANPIPES." Now I present "CLASSICAL REPERTOIRE FOR VIOLIN" with piano accompaniment. This work contains music which I adapted and arranged especially for the violin.

In my opinion classical music is the best basis for learning to play any instrument. Great performe have proven that the violin can be successfully used for playing not only classic music, but also symphonic or chamber music from classical, romantic, or modern periods just as well as any other instrument. No longer is the contemporary repertoire considered unfit for the violin.

Every sincere instrumentalist needs a regular study program. Daily practice of technical exercises and etudes is necessary for improving and maintaining the acquired results. Playing works of music regularly should be the aim of every musician (amateur as well as professional).

It has not been easy to find suitable and nice music for all levels. It was especially difficult finding simple melodies. I think that studying well-known melodies is both easy and enjoyable for the beginning player. I have carefully chosen the best keys for violin and therefore many songs are not in the keys in which they were originally written. Also, a number of other adaptations have been introduced to make the music more suitable for performance on the violin. The structure of the music has not been altered.

I hope you will find my "CLASSICAL REPERTOIRE FOR VIOLIN" not only instructive and useful, but also pleasant and entertaining.

Lots of success,

Delft
August 1996

COSTEL PUSCOIU

ABOUT THE AUTHOR

Costel Puscoiu was born on August 29, 1951, in Bucharest, Romania. He studied and graduated from the Ciprian Porumbescu College of Music in Bucharest, majoring in Composition and Theory. In Romania he worked as a music teacher, and for some years he was a conductor and researcher at the Institute for Ethnology and Folklore in Bucharest. He was also a member of the Society of Romanian Composers.

His compositions comprise symphonic music (symphonies, cantatas, concertos for viola), chamber music (string quartets, sonatas for clarinet and piano, contemporary pieces for several ensembles, music for pan flute), choir pieces, and film scores. His compositions are often influenced by Romanian folklore and Byzantine liturgies. He has also contributed to several musicological and folkloristic studies and articles.

In September of 1982 Puscoiu moved to the Netherlands from his native Romania; now he is working in the Music School department as a pan flute teacher and a leader of an orchestra at the Free Academy Westvest in Delft. Meanwhile he has become a member of the Dutch Composers Association.

CHILDREN'S SONG

WOLFGANG AMADEUS MOZART

TO JOY
(from Symphony no.9)

LUDWIG VAN BEETHOVEN

SAINT ANTHONY CHORALE

JOSEPH HAYDN

9

GAVOTTE

MICHAEL PRAETORIUS

FANFARE

A I R

WOLFGANG AMADEUS MOZART

MINUET

ANONYMOUS

GAVOTTE

GEORGE FRIEDRICH HANDEL

OH, TINY CHILD

JOHANN SEBASTIAN BACH

15

MINUET

JAMES HOOK

ANDANTINO

JEAN-BAPTISTE LULLY

BRUNETTE

JOSEPH BODIN DE BOISMORTIER

MARCH
(from "The Peasants' Cantata")

JOHANN SEBASTIAN BACH

Allegro moderato

18

MINUET
(from "Fireworks Music")

GEORGE FRIEDRICH HANDEL

MINUET
(from "Fireworks Music")

GEORGE FRIEDRICH HANDEL

Allegretto

BRANLE

JOSEPH BODIN DE BOISMORTIER

MELODY
(from "Album for the youth")

ROBERT SCHUMANN

RONDINO

JEAN PHILIPPE RAMEAU

BURLESQUE
(from "Music book for Wolfgang")

LEOPOLD MOZART

SCARBOROUGH FAIR

TRADITIONAL

Andantino grazioso

THE ROYAL MARCH OF THE LION

(from "Le carnaval des animaux")

CAMILLE SAINT-SAENS

28

ANDANTE

JOSEPH HAYDN

MICHAEL'S SONG

COSTEL PUSCOIU

ENGLISH DANCE

HENRY PURCELL

GAVOTTE

GEORGE FRIEDRICH HANDEL

IMPERTINENCE

George Friedrich Handel

TRUMPET AIR
(from "The Indian Queen")

DANIEL PURCELL

GREENSLEEVES

OLD ENGLISH SONG

PLAISIR D'AMOUR

JEAN PAUL MARTINI

CHORALE
(from Music book for Anna Magdalena Bach")

JOHANN SEBASTIAN BACH

MINUET

JOHANN KRIEGER

38

BECAUSE WE ARE CHEERFUL

VALENTIN RATHGEBER

ARIETTA

JOSEPH HAYDN

BOURREE

JOHANN KRIEGER

MINUET

Georg Philipp Telemann

ANDANTE
(from Brandenburg Concerto no.4)

JOHANN SEBASTIAN BACH

RONDEAU

JOSEPH BODIN DE BOISMORTIER

TAMBOURIN

JEAN PHILIPPE RAMEAU

MARCH
(from "Judas Maccabaeus")

GEORGE FRIEDRICH HANDEL

47

GAVOTTE

Allegretto

ESPRIT–PHILIPPE CHEDEVILLE

LULLABY

Andantino cantabile

JOHANNES BRAHMS

49

GAVOTTE

Andantino

GEORGE FRIEDRICH HANDEL

THEME FROM "SWANLAKE"

PIOTR ILICI TCHAYKOVSKY

LULLABY

WOLFGANG AMADEUS MOZART

Andante cantabile

GAVOTTE

ARCANGELO CORELLI

53

WALTZ

JOHANNES BRAHMS

MARTIAL AIR

Allegro moderato (Alla marcia)

HENRY PURCELL

MINUET
(from "Music book for Anna Magdalena Bach")

Allegretto

JOHANN SEBASTIAN BACH

58

SARABANDE

ARCANGELO CORELLI

Largo

MARCH
(from the "Occasional Oratorio")

GEORGE FRIEDRICH HANDEL

61

PANIS ANGELICUS

CESAR FRANCK

LARGO
(from Opera "Xerxes")

GEORGE FRIEDRICH HANDEL

66

BOURREE

(from Sonata no.2 in G major)

GEORGE FRIEDRICH HANDEL

MINUET
(from "Music book for Anna Magdalena Bach")

Allegretto

JOHANN SEBASTIAN BACH

MUSETTE 1
(from Sonata "La Persane")

PHILBERT DE LAVIGNE

Gracieusement

MUSETTE 2

AVE VERUM

WOLFGANG AMADEUS MOZART

MUSETTE 1 *D.C.*

Adagio

cresc. poco a poco

cresc. poco a poco

74

PRELUDIO
(from Sonata in A minor)

ARCANGELO CORELLI

MINUET

GEORG PHILIPP TELEMANN

BERCEUSE

GABRIEL FAURE

ALLEGRO
(from Brandenburg Concerto no.5)

JOHANN SEBASTIAN BACH

VIVACE

JEAN BAPTISTE LOEILLET DE GANT

(liscio)

THE PEACE
(from "Fireworks Music")

Largo alla Siciliana

GEORGE FRIEDRICH HANDEL

ALLEGRO
(from Brandenburg Concerto no.1)

JOHANN SEBASTIAN BACH

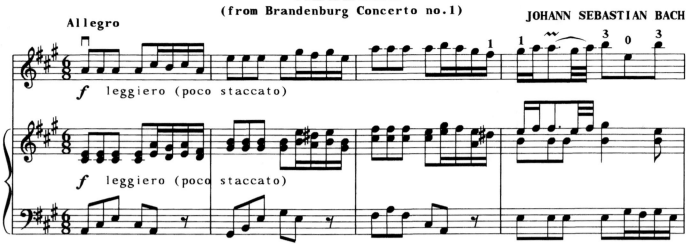

TRAUMEREI
(from "Children's scenes" op.15, no.7)

ROBERT SCHUMANN

POLOVETSIAN DANCE
(from opera "Tsar Igor")

Andantino cantabile
con espressione e dolce

ALEXANDER BORODIN